BIRDS of the NORTHWOODS

Activity Book

by David Grack

Adventure Publications, Inc.
Cambridge, Minnesota

I dedicate this book to my family: past, present and future.

A LETTER FROM THE AUTHOR

Dear Reader:

I love birds, and I enjoy sharing the thrills of bird watching. That is why I created *Birds of the Northwoods Activity Book*.

Birds are amazing creatures. They come in all shapes, sizes and colors. *Birds of the Northwoods Activity Book* celebrates the diversity of birds that inhabit the northeastern and north-central states. (See the map on the back cover.)

Birds may be small, but they can be seen and heard in most places. Some are hard to find. Others may be regular visitors to your neighborhood or home. Either way, you can use the activities in this book to learn fun facts about fifty birds from your area.

With people like you and me watching, we can better understand these creatures and their natural habitats. That is the first step to helping preserve these birds and their environments.

Enjoy *Birds of the Northwoods*, and have fun out there!

Sincerely,

David Grack

Cover and book design by Ryan Jacobson and Jonathan Norberg

Cover illustrations: Julie Martinez

Sample bird illustration by Jonathan Norberg. All other illustrations by Julie Martinez.

American Redstart and Hairy Woodpecker photos copyright Stan Tekiela. Eastern Wood Pewee photo copyright Maslowski Productions. Scarlet Tanager photo copyright Brian Collins. Yellow-bellied Sapsucker photo copyright Steve Mortensen. All other photos are copyright Shutterstock.

Edited by Ryan Jacobson

Special thanks to Anthony Hertzel for his technical review

10 9 8 7 6 5 4 3 2

Copyright 2007 by David Grack
Published by Adventure Publications, Inc.
820 Cleveland St. S
Cambridge, MN 55008
1-800-678-7006
www.adventurepublications.net
ISBN-13: 978-1-59193-166-9
ISBN-10: 1-59193-166-5

TABLE OF CONTENTS

INTRODUCTION

This book is designed to help you systematically observe, study and collect notes about 50 fascinating birds of the Northwoods. Hopefully, you will be prompted to learn more about each of these unique species by checking other resources; several are listed on page 64. We have also included some basic facts in the back so you can still complete the pages, even if you don't have access to other resources.

Birds of the Northwoods Activity Book is roughly organized by families, so you can compare one woodpecker to another and begin to learn the groupings used by bird scientists. The family groups are listed with the common name for each species in the Table of Contents. In addition, the scientific name is listed after the common name on each bird's individual page. Scientific names can be useful when searching reference books and the Internet.

Whether you are trying to identify a new bird, telling friends about birds you have seen or gathering information about a certain species, it also helps to know the proper terms for different parts of bird anatomy. The diagram below illustrates basic bird features. Because it represents the physical characteristics of many different birds, it shouldn't be confused with one particular species.

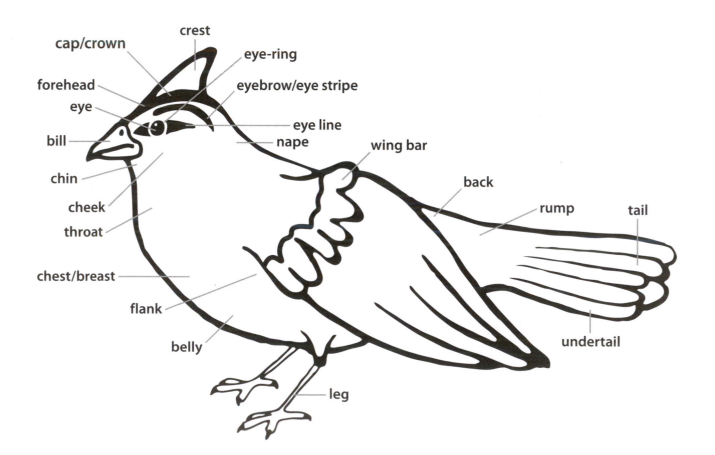

HOW TO USE THIS BOOK

For each species covered in this book you will be asked to color the bird, jot down a few interesting facts or personal observations, and answer several basic questions. Use the following notes—along with the Sample Page on page 7—as a guide to get started.

Coloring

Simply follow the key provided for each bird illustration to fill in the areas with the right colors. We've numbered them consistently, so "1" will always be black, and so on. The birds pictured are usually males since they are more colorful. Females have better camouflage because they often tend the nest, and being less noticeable helps them avoid predators.

Size

You can write in a specific size if you find one in another resource, or use the list on page 59. You can also fill in one of the circles based on your own observations as to whether it looks roughly the size of a sparrow, robin or crow.

Facts/Notes

You have lots of choices here. Make notes based on your observations or look up information in other resources. If you use your own observations, the questions below provide some helpful ideas on what to look for when watching birds.

1. What shape is the bird?
   a.) Is its head rounded, flat or peaked?
   b.) Is its tail forked or pointed?
   c.) Are its legs thick or thin?
   d.) Do its feet have large or small claws?
   e.) Is its beak thin or thick? Long or short? Straight or curved?

2. What are the bird's colors and field markings?
   a.) Is the bird one color or several different colors?
   b.) What is the main color?
   c.) Is there a pattern of color on its tail and/or wings?
   d.) Are there rings or stripes around its eyes?

3. What is the bird doing?
   a.) Does it interact with other birds?
   b.) Does it defend its territory?
   c.) Does it eat from a feeder? If so, what does it eat?

Range

Do you see the same types of birds all year? Your answer is probably no. Many birds change their locations by migrating—moving from one region to another during different seasons of the year. Some birds migrate great distances, from the Northwoods all the way to South America. Some travel just far enough to get away from extreme weather, such as the snow and cold of winter. Other birds stay in the same place all year. To answer this question, research range maps in other resource books (such as the ones listed on page 64) or check the Seasonal Bird Location chart that begins on page 60.

Habitat

For each species, you will be asked to check the appropriate box next to a picture of one of the three common habitats listed below. You can also sketch or color in a habitat setting where you could expect to see that type of bird. Reference books are great sources of information on birds' habitat needs, or you can use the list on page 59 of this book.

The environment where a bird makes its home is known as its habitat. Some birds are adaptable and can be found in different types of habitat, while others have more specific needs. A habitat must provide a bird and its family with the right resources for survival, including food, water, shelter and space. For instance, some birds eat insects while others eat berries. Habitats may be as small as your backyard or as large as several miles or more. The following are three general habitat types found in Northwoods states:

Woodland

Woodland habitat includes deciduous and coniferous forests; open forests that have a mixture of trees, shrubs and grass; and "edge" habitat where forest and grassland meet.

Grassland

Grasses and wildflowers are the dominant forms of plant life in this kind of habitat, although you may find a few shrubs and trees.

Wetland

Wetland habitat includes areas such as marshes, swamps and the shorelines of lakes and rivers.

COMMON NAME *Scientific name*

☑Check the box after you have seen this bird.

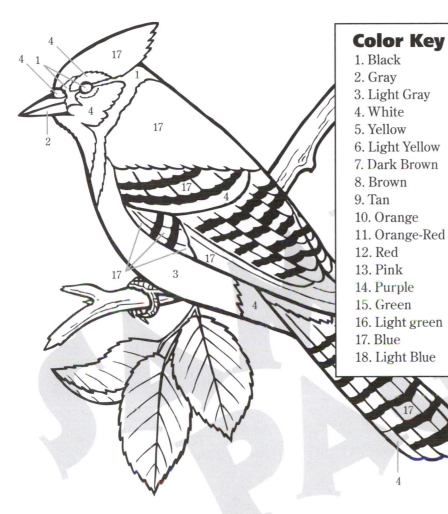

Color Key
1. Black
2. Gray
3. Light Gray
4. White
5. Yellow
6. Light Yellow
7. Dark Brown
8. Brown
9. Tan
10. Orange
11. Orange-Red
12. Red
13. Pink
14. Purple
15. Green
16. Light green
17. Blue
18. Light Blue

SIZE: ____12____ "

- ○ 17½ or larger
- ○ 17" (crow size)
- ● 11–16½"
- ○ 9–10½" (robin size)
- ○ 7–8½"
- ○ 5-6½" (sparrow size)
- ○ Less than 5"

FACTS/NOTES:

1. *Often seen in forests and at backyard feeders.*
2. *Eats insects, fruit, carrion, seeds and nuts.*
3. *Male and female work together to build the nest.*
4. *I saw one at my feeder in September.*
5. *Imitates the calls of other birds and caches its food.*

Range: At what time of year are you most likely to find this bird in your area?

A. Summer   **B.** Winter   Ⓒ **C.** All Year   **D.** Never

Draw a nearby spot where you might see this bird.

In which habitat is this bird most likely to nest?

☑ **Woodland**

☐ **Grassland**

☐ **Wetland**

BALTIMORE ORIOLE *Icterus galbula*

⬭ Check the box after you have seen this bird.

Color Key
1. Black
2. Gray
4. White
10. Orange

SIZE: _____ "

○ 17½" or larger

○ 17" (crow size)

○ 11–16½"

○ 9–10½" (robin size)

○ 7–8½"

○ 5-6½" (sparrow size)

○ Less than 5"

FACTS/NOTES:

1. _____

_____

2. _____

_____

3. _____

_____

4. _____

_____

5. _____

_____

Range: At what time of year are you most likely to find this bird in your area?

A. Summer   **B.** Winter   **C.** All Year   **D.** Never

In which habitat is this bird most likely to nest?

⬭ **Woodland**

⬭ **Grassland**

⬭ **Wetland**

Draw a nearby spot where you might see this bird.

BOBOLINK *Dolichonyx oryzivorus*

☐ Check the box after you have seen this bird.

Color Key
1. Black
2. Gray
4. White
5. Yellow
6. Light Yellow
7. Dark Brown
9. Tan

Range: At what time of year are you most likely to find this bird in your area?

A. Summer   **B.** Winter   **C.** All Year   **D.** Never

Draw a nearby spot where you might see this bird.

SIZE: _____ "

○ 17½" or larger

○ 17" (crow size)

○ 11–16½"

○ 9–10½" (robin size)

○ 7–8½"

○ 5-6½" (sparrow size)

○ Less than 5"

FACTS/NOTES:

1. _____

_____

2. _____

_____

3. _____

_____

4. _____

_____

5. _____

_____

In which habitat is this bird most likely to nest?

☐ **Woodland**

☐ **Grassland**

☐ **Wetland**

COMMON GRACKLE *Quiscalus quiscula*

◻ Check the box after you have seen this bird.

Color Key
1. Black
2. Gray
6. Light Yellow
7. Dark Brown
14. Purple

SIZE: _____ "

- ○ 17½" or larger
- ○ 17" (crow size)
- ○ 11–16½"
- ○ 9–10½" (robin size)
- ○ 7–8½"
- ○ 5-6½" (sparrow size)
- ○ Less than 5"

FACTS/NOTES:

1. _____
   _____
2. _____
   _____
3. _____
   _____
4. _____
   _____
5. _____
   _____

Range: At what time of year are you most likely to find this bird in your area?

A. Summer   **B.** Winter   **C.** All Year   **D.** Never

Draw a nearby spot where you might see this bird.

In which habitat is this bird most likely to nest?

◻ **Woodland**

◻ **Grassland**

◻ **Wetland**

EASTERN MEADOWLARK *Sturnella magna*

☐ Check the box after you have seen this bird.

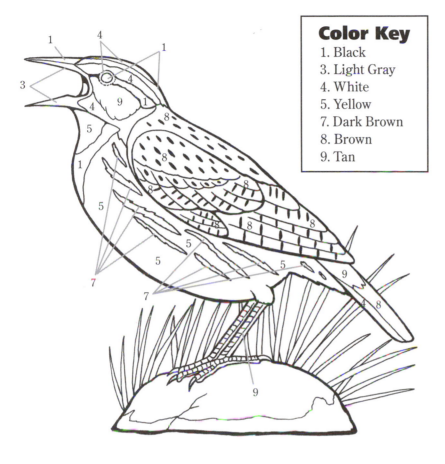

Color Key
1. Black
3. Light Gray
4. White
5. Yellow
7. Dark Brown
8. Brown
9. Tan

SIZE: _____ "

○ 17½" or larger
○ 17" (crow size)
○ 11–16½"
○ 9–10½" (robin size)
○ 7–8½"
○ 5-6½" (sparrow size)
○ Less than 5"

FACTS/NOTES:

1. _____
   _____
2. _____
   _____
3. _____
   _____
4. _____
   _____
5. _____
   _____

Range: At what time of year are you most likely to find this bird in your area?

A. Summer   **B.** Winter   **C.** All Year   **D.** Never

In which habitat is this bird most likely to nest?

☐ **Woodland**

☐ **Grassland**

☐ **Wetland**

Draw a nearby spot where you might see this bird.

RED-WINGED BLACKBIRD *Agelaius phoeniceus*

◯ Check the box after you have seen this bird.

Color Key
1. Black
5. Yellow
12. Red

SIZE: _____ "

O 17½" or larger

O 17" (crow size)

O 11–16½"

O 9–10½" (robin size)

O 7–8½"

O 5-6½" (sparrow size)

O Less than 5"

FACTS/NOTES:

1. _____

_____

2. _____

_____

3. _____

_____

4. _____

_____

5. _____

_____

Range: At what time of year are you most likely to find this bird in your area?

A. Summer **B.** Winter **C.** All Year **D.** Never

Draw a nearby spot where you might see this bird.

In which habitat is this bird most likely to nest?

◯ **Woodland**

◯ **Grassland**

◯ **Wetland**

12

AMERICAN TREE SPARROW *Spizella arborea*

⬜ Check the box after you have seen this bird.

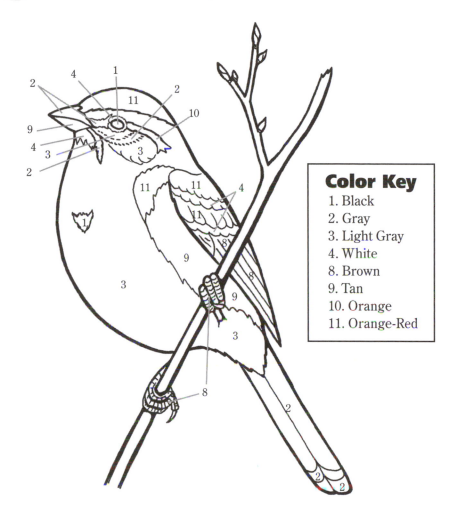

Color Key
1. Black
2. Gray
3. Light Gray
4. White
8. Brown
9. Tan
10. Orange
11. Orange-Red

SIZE: _____ "

○ 17½" or larger
○ 17" (crow size)
○ 11–16½"
○ 9–10½" (robin size)
○ 7–8½"
○ 5-6½" (sparrow size)
○ Less than 5"

FACTS/NOTES:

1. _____
_____
2. _____
_____
3. _____
_____
4. _____
_____
5. _____
_____

Range: At what time of year are you most likely to find this bird in your area?

A. Summer   **B.** Winter   **C.** All Year   **D.** Never

Draw a nearby spot where you might see this bird.

In which habitat is this bird most likely to nest?

⬜ **Woodland**

⬜ **Grassland**

⬜ **Wetland**

CHIPPING SPARROW *Spizella passerina*

⬜ Check the box after you have seen this bird.

Color Key
1. Black
2. Gray
3. Light Gray
4. White
8. Brown
9. Tan
11. Orange-Red

SIZE: _____ "

○ 17½" or larger

○ 17" (crow size)

○ 11–16½"

○ 9–10½" (robin size)

○ 7–8½"

○ 5-6½" (sparrow size)

○ Less than 5"

FACTS/NOTES:

1. _____

_____

2. _____

_____

3. _____

_____

4. _____

_____

5. _____

_____

Range: At what time of year are you most likely to find this bird in your area?

A. Summer   **B.** Winter   **C.** All Year   **D.** Never

In which habitat is this bird most likely to nest?

⬜ **Woodland**

⬜ **Grassland**

⬜ **Wetland**

Draw a nearby spot where you might see this bird.

DARK-EYED JUNCO *Junco hyemalis*

◯ Check the box after you have seen this bird.

Color Key
1. Black
2. Gray
4. White
13. Pink

SIZE: _____ "

- ◯ 17½" or larger
- ◯ 17" (crow size)
- ◯ 11–16½"
- ◯ 9–10½" (robin size)
- ◯ 7–8½"
- ◯ 5-6½" (sparrow size)
- ◯ Less than 5"

FACTS/NOTES:

1. _____

_____

2. _____

_____

3. _____

_____

4. _____

_____

5. _____

_____

Range: At what time of year are you most likely to find this bird in your area?

A. Summer **B.** Winter **C.** All Year **D.** Never

Draw a nearby spot where you might see this bird.

In which habitat is this bird most likely to nest?

◯ **Woodland**

◯ **Grassland**

◯ **Wetland**

15

EASTERN TOWHEE *Pipilo erythrophthalmus*

◯ Check the box after you have seen this bird.

Color Key
1. Black
2. Gray
4. White
8. Brown
11. Orange-Red
12. Red

SIZE: _____ "

○ 17½" or larger

○ 17" (crow size)

○ 11–16½"

○ 9–10½" (robin size)

○ 7–8½"

○ 5-6½" (sparrow size)

○ Less than 5"

FACTS/NOTES:

1. _____

_____

2. _____

_____

3. _____

_____

4. _____

_____

5. _____

_____

Range: At what time of year are you most likely to find this bird in your area?

A. Summer   **B.** Winter   **C.** All Year   **D.** Never

In which habitat is this bird most likely to nest?

◯ **Woodland**

◯ **Grassland**

◯ **Wetland**

Draw a nearby spot where you might see this bird.

16

HOUSE SPARROW *Passer domesticus*

◯ Check the box after you have seen this bird.

Color Key
1. Black
2. Gray
3. Light Gray
4. White
7. Dark Brown
8. Brown
9. Tan

SIZE: _____ "

○ 17½" or larger

○ 17" (crow size)

○ 11–16½"

○ 9–10½" (robin size)

○ 7–8½"

○ 5-6½" (sparrow size)

○ Less than 5"

FACTS/NOTES:

1. _____
   _____

2. _____
   _____

3. _____
   _____

4. _____
   _____

5. _____
   _____

Range: At what time of year are you most likely to find this bird in your area?

A. Summer   **B.** Winter   **C.** All Year   **D.** Never

Draw a nearby spot where you might see this bird.

In which habitat is this bird most likely to nest?

◯ **Woodland**

◯ **Grassland**

◯ **Wetland**

EVENING GROSBEAK *Coccothraustes vespertinus*

☐ Check the box after you have seen this bird.

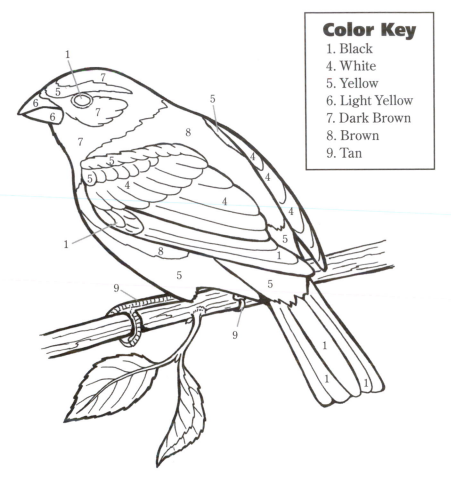

Color Key
1. Black
4. White
5. Yellow
6. Light Yellow
7. Dark Brown
8. Brown
9. Tan

SIZE: _____ "

○ 17½" or larger

○ 17" (crow size)

○ 11–16½"

○ 9–10½" (robin size)

○ 7–8½"

○ 5-6½" (sparrow size)

○ Less than 5"

FACTS/NOTES:

1. _____

_____

2. _____

_____

3. _____

_____

4. _____

_____

5. _____

_____

Range: At what time of year are you most likely to find this bird in your area?

A. Summer   **B.** Winter   **C.** All Year   **D.** Never

Draw a nearby spot where you might see this bird.

In which habitat is this bird most likely to nest?

☐ **Woodland**

☐ **Grassland**

☐ **Wetland**

NORTHERN CARDINAL *Cardinalis cardinalis*

☐ Check the box after you have seen this bird.

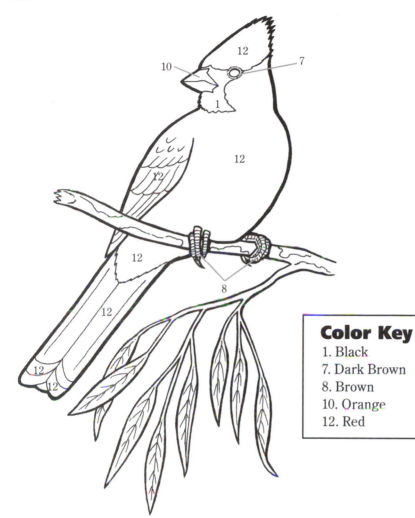

Color Key
1. Black
7. Dark Brown
8. Brown
10. Orange
12. Red

SIZE: _____ "

○ 17½" or larger

○ 17" (crow size)

○ 11–16½"

○ 9–10½" (robin size)

○ 7–8½"

○ 5-6½" (sparrow size)

○ Less than 5"

FACTS/NOTES:

1. _____

_____

2. _____

_____

3. _____

_____

4. _____

_____

5. _____

_____

Range: At what time of year are you most likely to find this bird in your area?

A. Summer   **B.** Winter   **C.** All Year   **D.** Never

In which habitat is this bird most likely to nest?

☐ **Woodland**

☐ **Grassland**

☐ **Wetland**

Draw a nearby spot where you might see this bird.

RED CROSSBILL *Loxia curvirostra*

Check the box after you have seen this bird.

Color Key
1. Black
4. White
7. Dark Brown
8. Brown
11. Orange-Red

SIZE: _____ "

- ○ 17½" or larger
- ○ 17" (crow size)
- ○ 11–16½"
- ○ 9–10½" (robin size)
- ○ 7–8½"
- ○ 5-6½" (sparrow size)
- ○ Less than 5"

FACTS/NOTES:

1. _____

   _____

2. _____

   _____

3. _____

   _____

4. _____

   _____

5. _____

   _____

Range: At what time of year are you most likely to find this bird in your area?

A. Summer **B.** Winter **C.** All Year **D.** Never

Draw a nearby spot where you might see this bird.

In which habitat is this bird most likely to nest?

☐ **Woodland**

☐ **Grassland**

☐ **Wetland**

ROSE-BREASTED GROSBEAK *Pheucticus ludovicianus*

☐ Check the box after you have seen this bird.

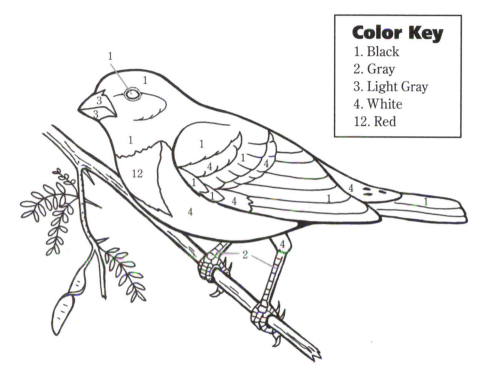

Color Key
1. Black
2. Gray
3. Light Gray
4. White
12. Red

SIZE: _____ "

○ 17½" or larger

○ 17" (crow size)

○ 11–16½"

○ 9–10½" (robin size)

○ 7–8½"

○ 5-6½" (sparrow size)

○ Less than 5"

FACTS/NOTES:

1. _____

_____

2. _____

_____

3. _____

_____

4. _____

_____

5. _____

_____

Range: At what time of year are you most likely to find this bird in your area?

A. Summer   **B.** Winter   **C.** All Year   **D.** Never

In which habitat is this bird most likely to nest?

☐ **Woodland**

☐ **Grassland**

☐ **Wetland**

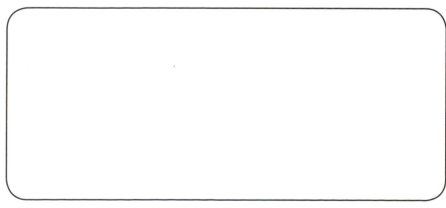

Draw a nearby spot where you might see this bird.

GRAY CATBIRD *Dumetella carolinensis*

○ Check the box after you have seen this bird.

Color Key
1. Black
2. Gray
11. Orange-Red

SIZE: _____ "

○ 17½" or larger

○ 17" (crow size)

○ 11–16½"

○ 9–10½" (robin size)

○ 7–8½"

○ 5-6½" (sparrow size)

○ Less than 5"

FACTS/NOTES:

1. _____

_____

2. _____

_____

3. _____

_____

4. _____

_____

5. _____

_____

Range: At what time of year are you most likely to find this bird in your area?

A. Summer   **B.** Winter   **C.** All Year   **D.** Never

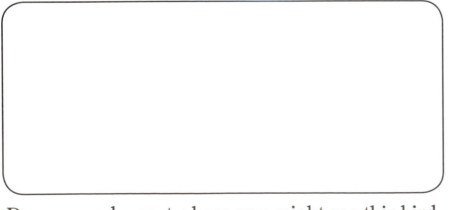

Draw a nearby spot where you might see this bird.

In which habitat is this bird most likely to nest?

○ **Woodland**

○ **Grassland**

○ **Wetland**

BLACK-CAPPED CHICKADEE *Poecile atricapillus*

☐ Check the box after you have seen this bird.

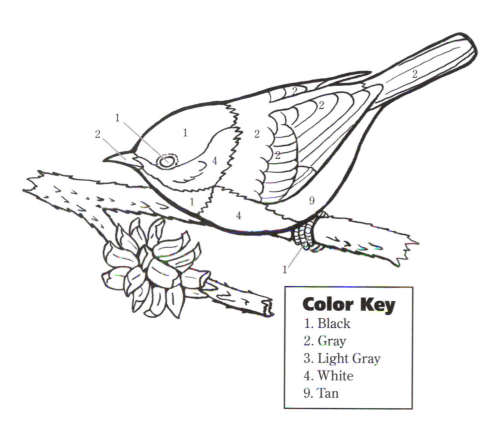

Color Key
1. Black
2. Gray
3. Light Gray
4. White
9. Tan

SIZE: _____ "

○ 17½" or larger

○ 17" (crow size)

○ 11–16½"

○ 9–10½" (robin size)

○ 7–8½"

○ 5-6½" (sparrow size)

○ Less than 5"

FACTS/NOTES:

1. _____

_____

2. _____

_____

3. _____

_____

4. _____

_____

5. _____

_____

Range: At what time of year are you most likely to find this bird in your area?

A. Summer   **B.** Winter   **C.** All Year   **D.** Never

Draw a nearby spot where you might see this bird.

In which habitat is this bird most likely to nest?

☐ **Woodland**

☐ **Grassland**

☐ **Wetland**

BROWN CREEPER *Certhia americana*

☐ Check the box after you have seen this bird.

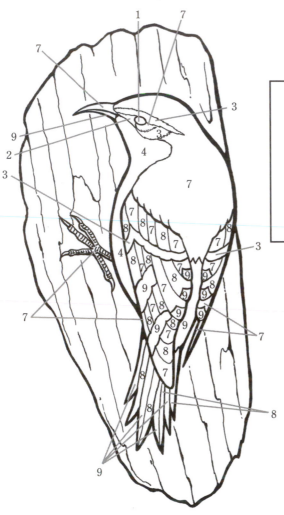

Color Key
1. Black
2. Gray
3. Light Gray
4. White
7. Dark Brown
8. Brown
9. Tan

SIZE: _____ "

- ○ 17½" or larger
- ○ 17" (crow size)
- ○ 11–16½"
- ○ 9–10½" (robin size)
- ○ 7–8½"
- ○ 5-6½" (sparrow size)
- ○ Less than 5"

FACTS/NOTES:

1. _____

_____

2. _____

_____

3. _____

_____

4. _____

_____

5. _____

_____

Range: At what time of year are you most likely to find this bird in your area?

A. Summer   **B.** Winter   **C.** All Year   **D.** Never

Draw a nearby spot where you might see this bird.

In which habitat is this bird most likely to nest?

☐ **Woodland**

☐ **Grassland**

☐ **Wetland**

AMERICAN CROW *Corvus brachyrhynchos*

☐ Check the box after you have seen this bird.

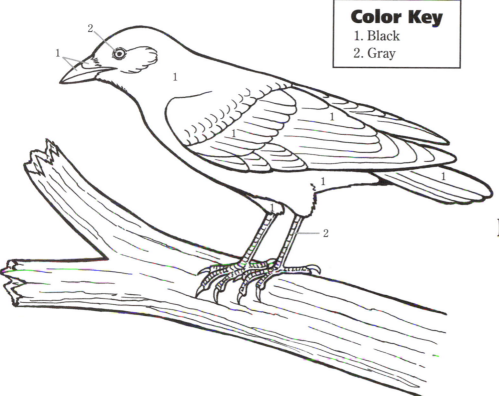

Color Key
1. Black
2. Gray

SIZE: _____ "

○ 17½" or larger
○ 17" (crow size)
○ 11–16½"
○ 9–10½" (robin size)
○ 7–8½"
○ 5-6½" (sparrow size)
○ Less than 5"

FACTS/NOTES:

1. _____
   _____
2. _____
   _____
3. _____
   _____
4. _____
   _____
5. _____
   _____

Range: At what time of year are you most likely to find this bird in your area?

A. Summer   **B.** Winter   **C.** All Year   **D.** Never

Draw a nearby spot where you might see this bird.

In which habitat is this bird most likely to nest?

☐ **Woodland**

☐ **Grassland**

☐ **Wetland**

BLUE JAY *Cyanocitta cristata*

○ Check the box after you have seen this bird.

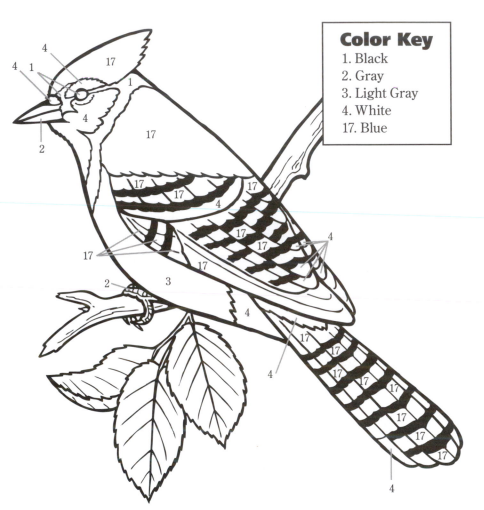

Color Key
1. Black
2. Gray
3. Light Gray
4. White
17. Blue

SIZE: _____ "

○ 17½" or larger

○ 17" (crow size)

○ 11–16½"

○ 9–10½" (robin size)

○ 7–8½"

○ 5-6½" (sparrow size)

○ Less than 5"

FACTS/NOTES:

1. _____

_____

2. _____

_____

3. _____

_____

4. _____

_____

5. _____

_____

Range: At what time of year are you most likely to find this bird in your area?

A. Summer   **B.** Winter   **C.** All Year   **D.** Never

Draw a nearby spot where you might see this bird.

In which habitat is this bird most likely to nest?

☐ **Woodland**

☐ **Grassland**

☐ **Wetland**

COMMON RAVEN *Corvus corax*

☐ Check the box after you have seen this bird.

Color Key
1. Black

SIZE: _____"

- ○ 17½" or larger
- ○ 17" (crow size)
- ○ 11–16½"
- ○ 9–10½" (robin size)
- ○ 7–8½"
- ○ 5-6½" (sparrow size)
- ○ Less than 5"

FACTS/NOTES:

1. _____
   _____
2. _____
   _____
3. _____
   _____
4. _____
   _____
5. _____
   _____

Range: At what time of year are you most likely to find this bird in your area?

A. Summer   **B.** Winter   **C.** All Year   **D.** Never

Draw a nearby spot where you might see this bird.

In which habitat is this bird most likely to nest?

☐ **Woodland**

☐ **Grassland**

☐ **Wetland**

27

MOURNING DOVE *Zenaida macroura*

○ Check the box after you have seen this bird.

Color Key
1. Black
2. Gray
4. White
7. Dark Brown
8. Brown
9. Tan
10. Orange
13. Pink
18. Light Blue

SIZE: _____"

○ 17½" or larger

○ 17" (crow size)

○ 11–16½"

○ 9–10½" (robin size)

○ 7–8½"

○ 5-6½" (sparrow size)

○ Less than 5"

FACTS/NOTES:

1. _____

_____

2. _____

_____

3. _____

_____

4. _____

_____

5. _____

_____

Range: At what time of year are you most likely to find this bird in your area?

A. Summer   **B.** Winter   **C.** All Year   **D.** Never

Draw a nearby spot where you might see this bird.

In which habitat is this bird most likely to nest?

☐ **Woodland**

☐ **Grassland**

☐ **Wetland**

AMERICAN GOLDFINCH *Carduelis tristis*

☐ Check the box after you have seen this bird.

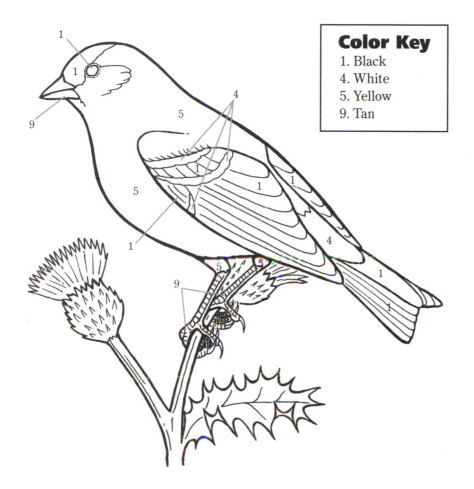

Color Key
1. Black
4. White
5. Yellow
9. Tan

○ 17½" or larger

○ 17" (crow size)

○ 11–16½"

○ 9–10½" (robin size)

○ 7–8½"

○ 5-6½" (sparrow size)

○ Less than 5"

FACTS/NOTES:

1. _____

_____

2. _____

_____

3. _____

_____

4. _____

_____

5. _____

_____

Range: At what time of year are you most likely to find this bird in your area?

A. Summer   **B.** Winter   **C.** All Year   **D.** Never

Draw a nearby spot where you might see this bird.

In which habitat is this bird most likely to nest?

☐ **Woodland**

☐ **Grassland**

☐ **Wetland**

HOUSE FINCH *Carpodacus mexicanus*

⬜ Check the box after you have seen this bird.

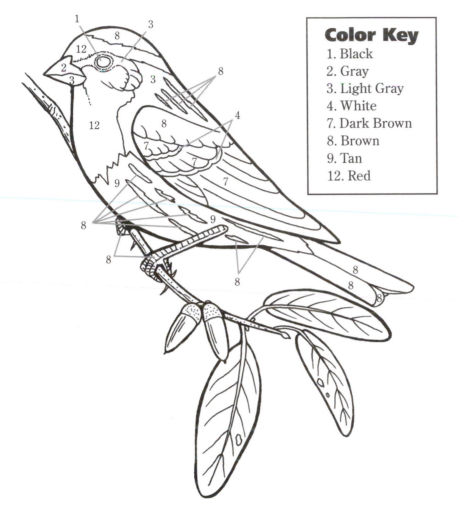

Color Key
1. Black
2. Gray
3. Light Gray
4. White
7. Dark Brown
8. Brown
9. Tan
12. Red

SIZE: _____ "

○ 17½" or larger

○ 17" (crow size)

○ 11–16½"

○ 9–10½" (robin size)

○ 7–8½"

○ 5-6½" (sparrow size)

○ Less than 5"

FACTS/NOTES:

1. _____

_____

2. _____

_____

3. _____

_____

4. _____

_____

5. _____

_____

Range: At what time of year are you most likely to find this bird in your area?

A. Summer   **B.** Winter   **C.** All Year   **D.** Never

In which habitat is this bird most likely to nest?

⬜ **Woodland**

⬜ **Grassland**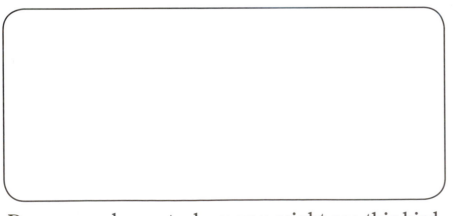

⬜ **Wetland**

Draw a nearby spot where you might see this bird.

PURPLE FINCH *Carpodacus purpureus*

◯ Check the box after you have seen this bird.

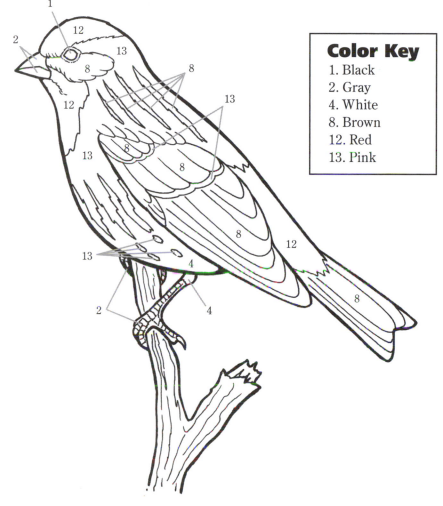

Color Key
1. Black
2. Gray
4. White
8. Brown
12. Red
13. Pink

SIZE: _____"

- ◯ 17½" or larger
- ◯ 17" (crow size)
- ◯ 11–16½"
- ◯ 9–10½" (robin size)
- ◯ 7–8½"
- ◯ 5-6½" (sparrow size)
- ◯ Less than 5"

FACTS/NOTES:

1. _____

   _____

2. _____

   _____

3. _____

   _____

4. _____

   _____

5. _____

   _____

Range: At what time of year are you most likely to find this bird in your area?

A. Summer   **B.** Winter   **C.** All Year   **D.** Never

Draw a nearby spot where you might see this bird.

In which habitat is this bird most likely to nest?

◯ **Woodland**

◯ **Grassland**

◯ **Wetland**

31

EASTERN KINGBIRD *Tyrannus tyrannus*

◯ Check the box after you have seen this bird.

Color Key
1. Black
2. Gray
4. White

SIZE: _____"

- ◯ 17½" or larger
- ◯ 17" (crow size)
- ◯ 11–16½"
- ◯ 9–10½" (robin size)
- ◯ 7–8½"
- ◯ 5-6½" (sparrow size)
- ◯ Less than 5"

FACTS/NOTES:

1. _____

_____

2. _____

_____

3. _____

_____

4. _____

_____

5. _____

_____

Range: At what time of year are you most likely to find this bird in your area?

A. Summer   **B.** Winter   **C.** All Year   **D.** Never

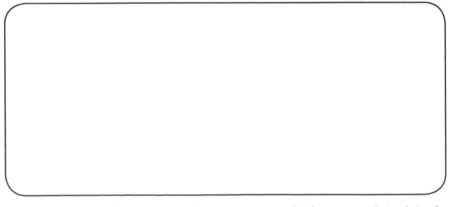

Draw a nearby spot where you might see this bird.

In which habitat is this bird most likely to nest?

◯ **Woodland**

◯ **Grassland**

◯ **Wetland**

32

EASTERN PHOEBE *Sayornis phoebe*

☐ Check the box after you have seen this bird.

Color Key
1. Black
2. Gray
3. Light Gray
4. White
6. Light Yellow

SIZE: _____ "

○ 17½" or larger
○ 17" (crow size)
○ 11–16½"
○ 9–10½" (robin size)
○ 7–8½"
○ 5-6½" (sparrow size)
○ Less than 5"

FACTS/NOTES:

1. _____
   _____
2. _____
   _____
3. _____
   _____
4. _____
   _____
5. _____
   _____

Range: At what time of year are you most likely to find this bird in your area?

A. Summer   **B.** Winter   **C.** All Year   **D.** Never

Draw a nearby spot where you might see this bird.

In which habitat is this bird most likely to nest?

☐ **Woodland**

☐ **Grassland**

☐ **Wetland**

EASTERN WOOD PEWEE *Contopus virens*

◯ Check the box after you have seen this bird.

Color Key
1. Black
2. Gray
3. Light Gray
4. White
10. Orange

SIZE: _____ "

- ◯ 17½" or larger
- ◯ 17" (crow size)
- ◯ 11–16½"
- ◯ 9–10½" (robin size)
- ◯ 7–8½"
- ◯ 5-6½" (sparrow size)
- ◯ Less than 5"

FACTS/NOTES:

1. _____

_____

2. _____

_____

3. _____

_____

4. _____

_____

5. _____

_____

Range: At what time of year are you most likely to find this bird in your area?

A. Summer   **B.** Winter   **C.** All Year   **D.** Never

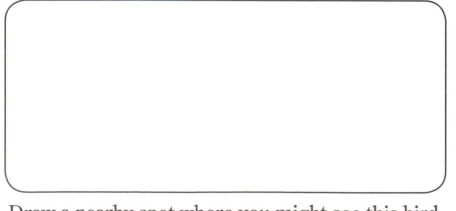

Draw a nearby spot where you might see this bird.

In which habitat is this bird most likely to nest?

◯ **Woodland**

◯ **Grassland**

◯ **Wetland**

RUBY-THROATED HUMMINGBIRD *Archilochus colubris*

⬜ Check the box after you have seen this bird.

Color Key
1. Black
2. Gray
4. White
12. Red
15. Green
16. Light green

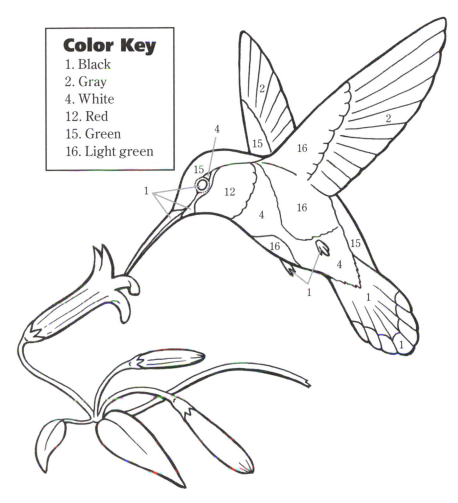

Range: At what time of year are you most likely to find this bird in your area?

A. Summer   **B.** Winter   **C.** All Year   **D.** Never

Draw a nearby spot where you might see this bird.

SIZE: _____ "

○ 17½" or larger

○ 17" (crow size)

○ 11–16½"

○ 9–10½" (robin size)

○ 7–8½"

○ 5-6½" (sparrow size)

○ Less than 5"

FACTS/NOTES:

1. _____

_____

2. _____

_____

3. _____

_____

4. _____

_____

5. _____

_____

In which habitat is this bird most likely to nest?

⬜ **Woodland**

⬜ **Grassland**

⬜ **Wetland**

BELTED KINGFISHER *Ceryle alcyon*

⬭ Check the box after you have seen this bird.

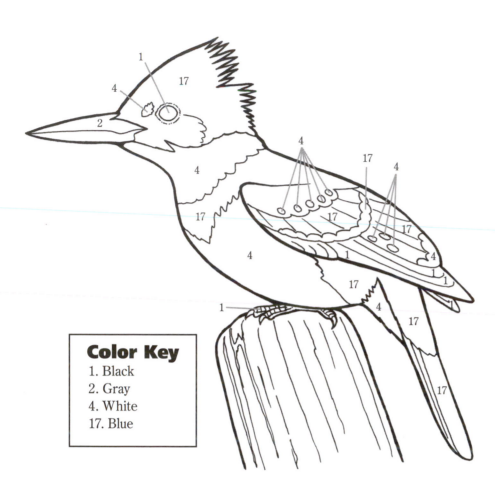

Color Key
1. Black
2. Gray
4. White
17. Blue

SIZE: _____ "

○ 17½" or larger
○ 17" (crow size)
○ 11–16½"
○ 9–10½" (robin size)
○ 7–8½"
○ 5-6½" (sparrow size)
○ Less than 5"

FACTS/NOTES:

1. _____
_____
2. _____
_____
3. _____
_____
4. _____
_____
5. _____
_____

Range: At what time of year are you most likely to find this bird in your area?

A. Summer   **B.** Winter   **C.** All Year   **D.** Never

Draw a nearby spot where you might see this bird.

In which habitat is this bird most likely to nest?

⬭ **Woodland**

⬭ **Grassland**

⬭ **Wetland**

RED-BREASTED NUTHATCH *Sitta canadensis*

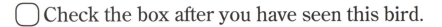

☐ Check the box after you have seen this bird.

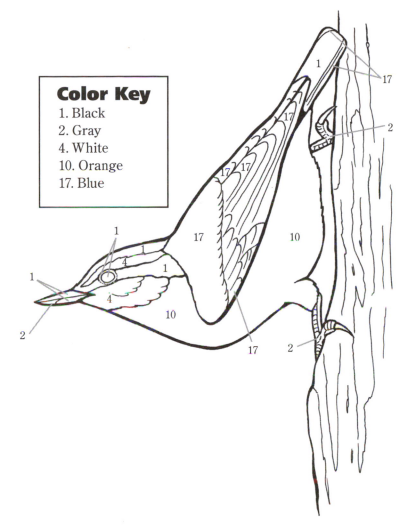

Color Key
1. Black
2. Gray
4. White
10. Orange
17. Blue

SIZE: _____ "

- ○ 17½" or larger
- ○ 17" (crow size)
- ○ 11–16½"
- ○ 9–10½" (robin size)
- ○ 7–8½"
- ○ 5-6½" (sparrow size)
- ○ Less than 5"

FACTS/NOTES:

1. _____
   _____
2. _____
   _____
3. _____
   _____
4. _____
   _____
5. _____
   _____

Range: At what time of year are you most likely to find this bird in your area?

A. Summer   **B.** Winter   **C.** All Year   **D.** Never

Draw a nearby spot where you might see this bird.

In which habitat is this bird most likely to nest?

☐ **Woodland**

☐ **Grassland**

☐ **Wetland**

WHITE-BREASTED NUTHATCH *Sitta carolinensis*

☐ Check the box after you have seen this bird.

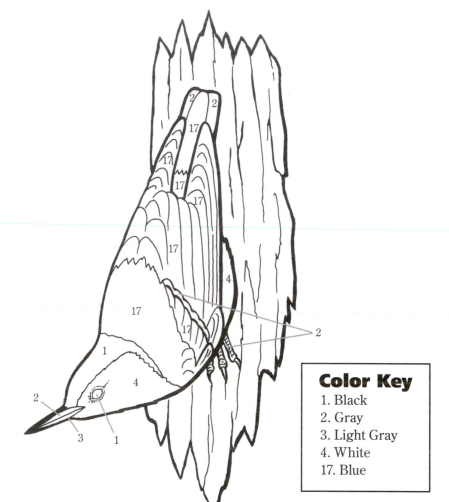

Color Key
1. Black
2. Gray
3. Light Gray
4. White
17. Blue

Range: At what time of year are you most likely to find this bird in your area?

A. Summer   **B.** Winter   **C.** All Year   **D.** Never

SIZE: _____"

○ 17½" or larger

○ 17" (crow size)

○ 11–16½"

○ 9–10½" (robin size)

○ 7–8½"

○ 5-6½" (sparrow size)

○ Less than 5"

FACTS/NOTES:

1. _____

_____

2. _____

_____

3. _____

_____

4. _____

_____

5. _____

_____

In which habitat is this bird most likely to nest?

☐ **Woodland**

☐ **Grassland**

☐ **Wetland**

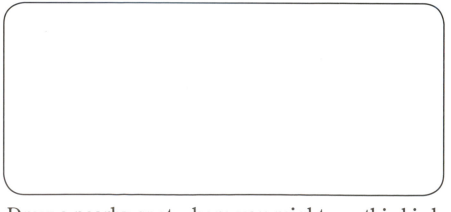

Draw a nearby spot where you might see this bird.

KILLDEER *Charadrius vociferus*

☐ Check the box after you have seen this bird.

Color Key
1. Black
4. White
8. Brown
9. Tan
10. Orange

SIZE: _____ "

- ○ 17½" or larger
- ○ 17" (crow size)
- ○ 11–16½"
- ○ 9–10½" (robin size)
- ○ 7–8½"
- ○ 5-6½" (sparrow size)
- ○ Less than 5"

FACTS/NOTES:

1. _____

_____

2. _____

_____

3. _____

_____

4. _____

_____

5. _____

_____

Range: At what time of year are you most likely to find this bird in your area?

A. Summer   **B.** Winter   **C.** All Year   **D.** Never

Draw a nearby spot where you might see this bird.

In which habitat is this bird most likely to nest?

☐ **Woodland**

☐ **Grassland**

☐ **Wetland**

BARN SWALLOW *Hirundo rustica*

◯ Check the box after you have seen this bird.

17

17

17

17

2

17

10

17

17

4

10

17

11

10

11

1

Color Key
1. Black
2. Gray
4. White
10. Orange
11. Orange-Red
17. Blue

SIZE: _____ "

O 17½" or larger

O 17" (crow size)

O 11–16½"

O 9–10½" (robin size)

O 7–8½"

O 5-6½" (sparrow size)

O Less than 5"

FACTS/NOTES:

1. _____

_____

2. _____

_____

3. _____

_____

4. _____

_____

5. _____

_____

Range: At what time of year are you most likely to find this bird in your area?

A. Summer   **B.** Winter   **C.** All Year   **D.** Never

In which habitat is this bird most likely to nest?

◯ **Woodland**

◯ **Grassland**

◯ **Wetland**

Draw a nearby spot where you might see this bird.

PURPLE MARTIN *Progne subis*

⬜ Check the box after you have seen this bird.

Color Key
1. Black
17. Blue

SIZE: _____ "

- ○ 17½" or larger
- ○ 17" (crow size)
- ○ 11–16½"
- ○ 9–10½" (robin size)
- ○ 7–8½"
- ○ 5-6½" (sparrow size)
- ○ Less than 5"

FACTS/NOTES:

1. _____

_____

2. _____

_____

3. _____

_____

4. _____

_____

5. _____

_____

Range: At what time of year are you most likely to find this bird in your area?

A. Summer **B.** Winter **C.** All Year **D.** Never

Draw a nearby spot where you might see this bird.

In which habitat is this bird most likely to nest?

⬜ **Woodland**

⬜ **Grassland**

⬜ **Wetland**

TREE SWALLOW *Tachycineta bicolor*

◯ Check the box after you have seen this bird.

Color Key
1. Black
4. White
7. Dark Brown
15. Green

SIZE: _____ "

- ◯ 17½" or larger
- ◯ 17" (crow size)
- ◯ 11–16½"
- ◯ 9–10½" (robin size)
- ◯ 7–8½"
- ◯ 5-6½" (sparrow size)
- ◯ Less than 5"

FACTS/NOTES:

1. _____

   _____

2. _____

   _____

3. _____

   _____

4. _____

   _____

5. _____

   _____

Range: At what time of year are you most likely to find this bird in your area?

A. Summer **B.** Winter **C.** All Year **D.** Never

Draw a nearby spot where you might see this bird.

In which habitat is this bird most likely to nest?

◯ **Woodland**

◯ **Grassland**

◯ **Wetland**

SCARLET TANAGER *Piranga olivacea*

☐ Check the box after you have seen this bird.

Color Key
1. Black
2. Gray
12. Red

SIZE: _____ "

- ○ 17½" or larger
- ○ 17" (crow size)
- ○ 11–16½"
- ○ 9–10½" (robin size)
- ○ 7–8½"
- ○ 5-6½" (sparrow size)
- ○ Less than 5"

FACTS/NOTES:

1. _____

_____

2. _____

_____

3. _____

_____

4. _____

_____

5. _____

_____

Range: At what time of year are you most likely to find this bird in your area?

A. Summer   **B.** Winter   **C.** All Year   **D.** Never

Draw a nearby spot where you might see this bird.

In which habitat is this bird most likely to nest?

☐ **Woodland**

☐ **Grassland**

☐ **Wetland**

AMERICAN ROBIN *Turdus migratorius*

⬜ Check the box after you have seen this bird.

Color Key
1. Black
2. Gray
4. White
5. Yellow
8. Brown
11. Orange-Red

SIZE: _____ "

○ 17½" or larger

○ 17" (crow size)

○ 11–16½"

○ 9–10½" (robin size)

○ 7–8½"

○ 5-6½" (sparrow size)

○ Less than 5"

FACTS/NOTES:

1. _____

_____

2. _____

_____

3. _____

_____

4. _____

_____

5. _____

_____

Range: At what time of year are you most likely to find this bird in your area?

A. Summer   **B.** Winter   **C.** All Year   **D.** Never

Draw a nearby spot where you might see this bird.

In which habitat is this bird most likely to nest?

⬜ **Woodland**

⬜ **Grassland**

⬜ **Wetland**

44

EASTERN BLUEBIRD *Sialia sialis*

⬜ Check the box after you have seen this bird.

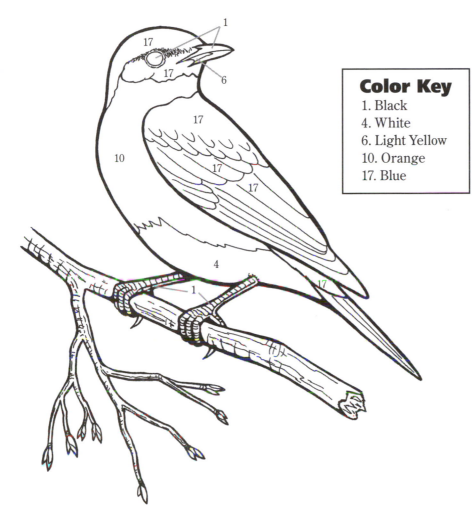

Color Key
1. Black
4. White
6. Light Yellow
10. Orange
17. Blue

SIZE: _____ "

○ 17½" or larger
○ 17" (crow size)
○ 11–16½"
○ 9–10½" (robin size)
○ 7–8½"
○ 5-6½" (sparrow size)
○ Less than 5"

FACTS/NOTES:

1. _____
   _____
2. _____
   _____
3. _____
   _____
4. _____
   _____
5. _____
   _____

Range: At what time of year are you most likely to find this bird in your area?

A. Summer   **B.** Winter   **C.** All Year   **D.** Never

Draw a nearby spot where you might see this bird.

In which habitat is this bird most likely to nest?

⬜ **Woodland**

⬜ **Grassland**

⬜ **Wetland**

AMERICAN REDSTART *Setophaga ruticilla*

⬜ Check the box after you have seen this bird.

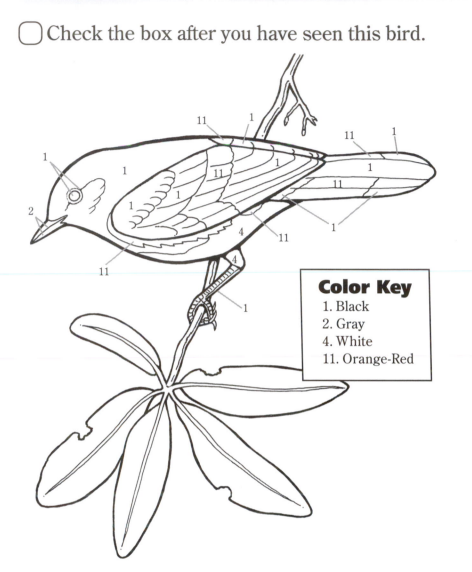

Color Key
1. Black
2. Gray
4. White
11. Orange-Red

SIZE: _____ "

○ 17½" or larger

○ 17" (crow size)

○ 11–16½"

○ 9–10½" (robin size)

○ 7–8½"

○ 5-6½" (sparrow size)

○ Less than 5"

FACTS/NOTES:

1. _____

_____

2. _____

_____

3. _____

_____

4. _____

_____

5. _____

_____

Range: At what time of year are you most likely to find this bird in your area?

A. Summer   **B.** Winter   **C.** All Year   **D.** Never

In which habitat is this bird most likely to nest?

⬜ **Woodland**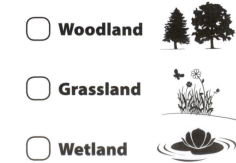

⬜ **Grassland**

⬜ **Wetland**

Draw a nearby spot where you might see this bird.

COMMON YELLOWTHROAT *Geothlypis trichas*

☐ Check the box after you have seen this bird.

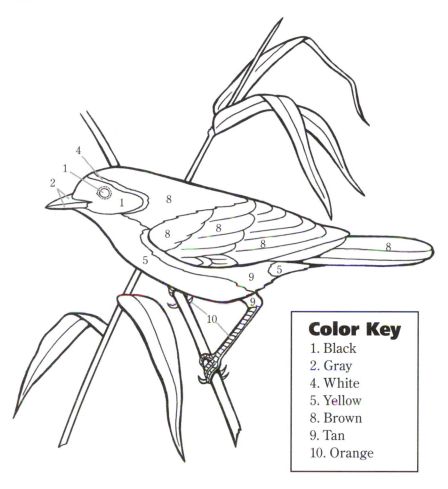

Color Key
1. Black
2. Gray
4. White
5. Yellow
8. Brown
9. Tan
10. Orange

Range: At what time of year are you most likely to find this bird in your area?

A. Summer   **B.** Winter   **C.** All Year   **D.** Never

Draw a nearby spot where you might see this bird.

SIZE: _____ "

○ 17½" or larger
○ 17" (crow size)
○ 11–16½"
○ 9–10½" (robin size)
○ 7–8½"
○ 5-6½" (sparrow size)
○ Less than 5"

FACTS/NOTES:

1. _____
   _____
2. _____
   _____
3. _____
   _____
4. _____
   _____
5. _____
   _____

In which habitat is this bird most likely to nest?

☐ **Woodland**

☐ **Grassland**

☐ **Wetland**

YELLOW WARBLER *Dendroica petechia*

⬜ Check the box after you have seen this bird.

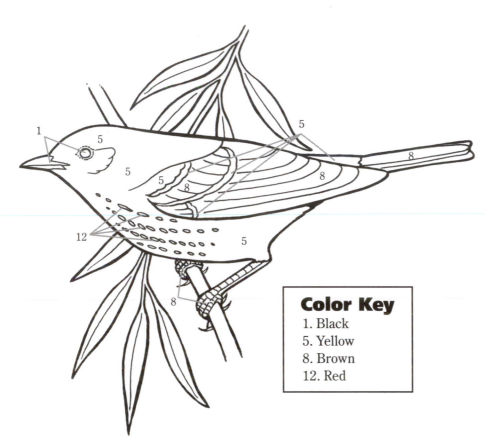

Color Key
1. Black
5. Yellow
8. Brown
12. Red

SIZE: _____ "

- ○ 17½" or larger
- ○ 17" (crow size)
- ○ 11–16½"
- ○ 9–10½" (robin size)
- ○ 7–8½"
- ○ 5-6½" (sparrow size)
- ○ Less than 5"

FACTS/NOTES:

1. _____

   _____

2. _____

   _____

3. _____

   _____

4. _____

   _____

5. _____

   _____

Range: At what time of year are you most likely to find this bird in your area?

A. Summer **B.** Winter **C.** All Year **D.** Never

In which habitat is this bird most likely to nest?

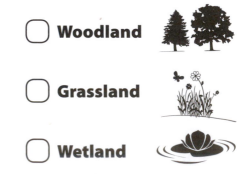

⬜ **Woodland**

⬜ **Grassland**

⬜ **Wetland**

Draw a nearby spot where you might see this bird.

YELLOW-RUMPED WARBLER *Dendroica coronata*

⬜ Check the box after you have seen this bird.

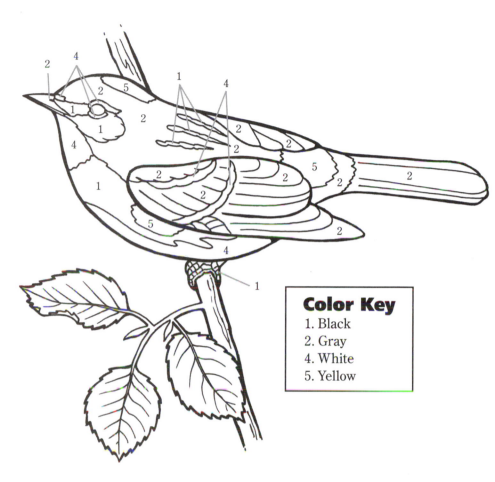

Color Key
1. Black
2. Gray
4. White
5. Yellow

Range: At what time of year are you most likely to find this bird in your area?

A. Summer　**B.** Winter　**C.** All Year　**D.** Never

Draw a nearby spot where you might see this bird.

SIZE: _____ "

○ 17½" or larger
○ 17" (crow size)
○ 11–16½"
○ 9–10½" (robin size)
○ 7–8½"
○ 5-6½" (sparrow size)
○ Less than 5"

FACTS/NOTES:

1. _____
_____
2. _____
_____
3. _____
_____
4. _____
_____
5. _____
_____

In which habitat is this bird most likely to nest?

⬜ **Woodland**

⬜ **Grassland**

⬜ **Wetland**

49

CEDAR WAXWING *Bombycilla cedrorum*

◯ Check the box after you have seen this bird.

Color Key
1. Black
2. Gray
3. Light Gray
4. White
5. Yellow
6. Light Yellow
8. Brown
12. Red

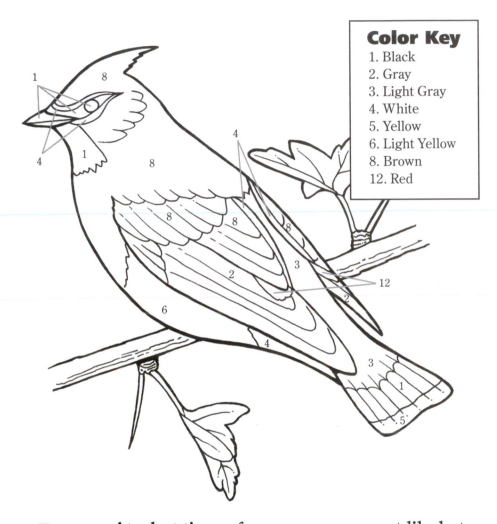

SIZE: _____ "

- ◯ 17½" or larger
- ◯ 17" (crow size)
- ◯ 11–16½"
- ◯ 9–10½" (robin size)
- ◯ 7–8½"
- ◯ 5-6½" (sparrow size)
- ◯ Less than 5"

FACTS/NOTES:

1. _____

_____

2. _____

_____

3. _____

_____

4. _____

_____

5. _____

_____

Range: At what time of year are you most likely to find this bird in your area?

A. Summer   **B.** Winter   **C.** All Year   **D.** Never

Draw a nearby spot where you might see this bird.

In which habitat is this bird most likely to nest?

◯ **Woodland**

◯ **Grassland**

◯ **Wetland**

DOWNY WOODPECKER *Picoides pubescens*

☐ Check the box after you have seen this bird.

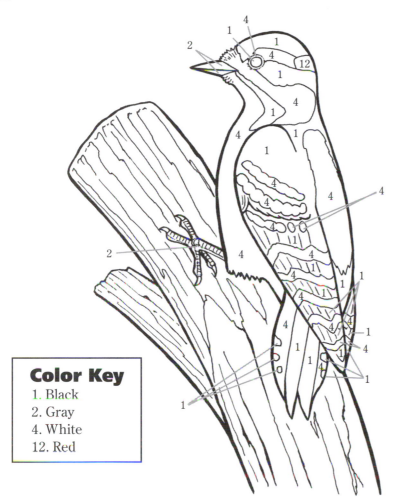

Color Key
1. Black
2. Gray
4. White
12. Red

Range: At what time of year are you most likely to find this bird in your area?

A. Summer   **B.** Winter   **C.** All Year   **D.** Never

Draw a nearby spot where you might see this bird.

SIZE: _____ "

O 17½" or larger

O 17" (crow size)

O 11–16½"

O 9–10½" (robin size)

O 7–8½"

O 5-6½" (sparrow size)

O Less than 5"

FACTS/NOTES:

1. _____

_____

2. _____

_____

3. _____

_____

4. _____

_____

5. _____

_____

In which habitat is this bird most likely to nest?

☐ **Woodland**

☐ **Grassland**

☐ **Wetland**

HAIRY WOODPECKER *Picoides villosus*

⬡ Check the box after you have seen this bird.

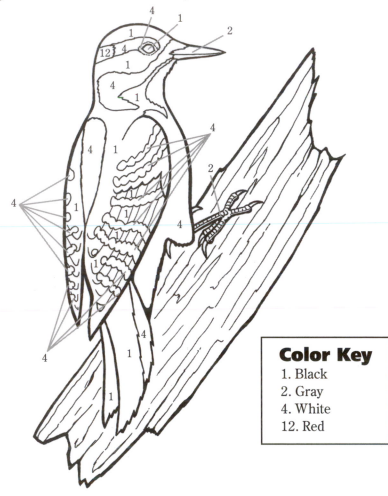

Color Key
1. Black
2. Gray
4. White
12. Red

SIZE: _____ "

○ 17½" or larger

○ 17" (crow size)

○ 11–16½"

○ 9–10½" (robin size)

○ 7–8½"

○ 5-6½" (sparrow size)

○ Less than 5"

FACTS/NOTES:

1. _____

_____

2. _____

_____

3. _____

_____

4. _____

_____

5. _____

_____

Range: At what time of year are you most likely to find this bird in your area?

A. Summer   **B.** Winter   **C.** All Year   **D.** Never

Draw a nearby spot where you might see this bird.

In which habitat is this bird most likely to nest?

⬡ **Woodland**

⬡ **Grassland**

⬡ **Wetland**

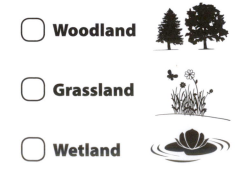

NORTHERN FLICKER *Colaptes auratus*

☐ Check the box after you have seen this bird.

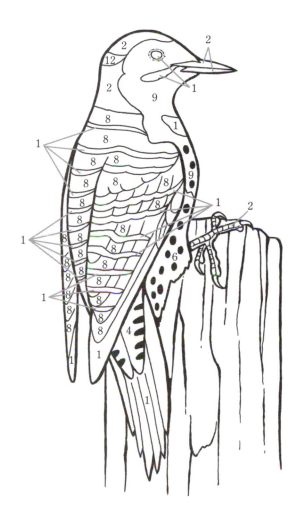

Color Key
1. Black
2. Gray
4. White
6. Light Yellow
8. Brown
9. Tan
12. Red

SIZE: _____ "

○ 17½" or larger

○ 17" (crow size)

○ 11–16½"

○ 9–10½" (robin size)

○ 7–8½"

○ 5-6½" (sparrow size)

○ Less than 5"

FACTS/NOTES:

1. _____

   _____

2. _____

   _____

3. _____

   _____

4. _____

   _____

5. _____

   _____

Range: At what time of year are you most likely to find this bird in your area?

A. Summer   **B.** Winter   **C.** All Year   **D.** Never

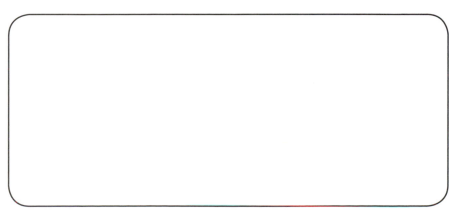

Draw a nearby spot where you might see this bird.

In which habitat is this bird most likely to nest?

☐ **Woodland**

☐ **Grassland**

☐ **Wetland**

PILEATED WOODPECKER *Dryocopus pileatus*

◯ Check the box after you have seen this bird.

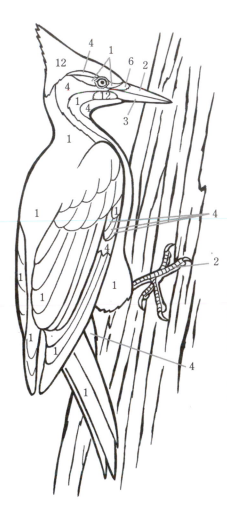

Color Key
1. Black
2. Gray
3. Light Gray
4. White
6. Light Yellow
12. Red

○ 17½" or larger

○ 17" (crow size)

○ 11–16½"

○ 9–10½" (robin size)

○ 7–8½"

○ 5-6½" (sparrow size)

○ Less than 5"

FACTS/NOTES:

1. _____

_____

2. _____

_____

3. _____

_____

4. _____

_____

5. _____

_____

Range: At what time of year are you most likely to find this bird in your area?

A. Summer **B.** Winter **C.** All Year **D.** Never

In which habitat is this bird most likely to nest?

◯ **Woodland**

◯ **Grassland**

◯ **Wetland**

Draw a nearby spot where you might see this bird.

RED-HEADED WOODPECKER *Melanerpes erythrocephalus*

⬜ Check the box after you have seen this bird.

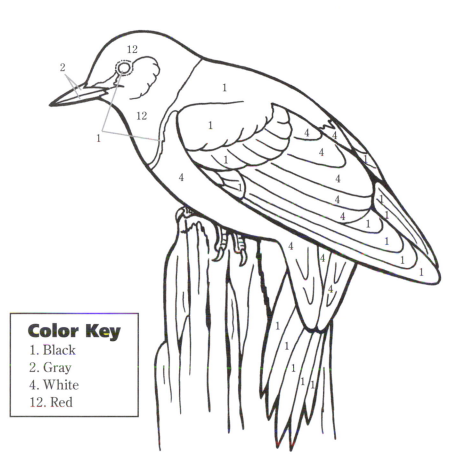

Color Key
1. Black
2. Gray
4. White
12. Red

Range: At what time of year are you most likely to find this bird in **your area**?

A. Summer   **B.** Winter   **C.** All Year   **D.** Never

Draw a nearby spot where you might see this bird.

SIZE: _____ "

○ 17½" or larger

○ 17" (crow size)

○ 11–16½"

○ 9–10½" (robin size)

○ 7–8½"

○ 5-6½" (sparrow size)

○ Less than 5"

FACTS/NOTES:

1. _____

_____

2. _____

_____

3. _____

_____

4. _____

_____

5. _____

_____

In which habitat is this bird most likely to nest?

⬜ **Woodland**

⬜ **Grassland**

⬜ **Wetland**

55

YELLOW-BELLIED SAPSUCKER *Sphyrapicus varius*

☐ Check the box after you have seen this bird.

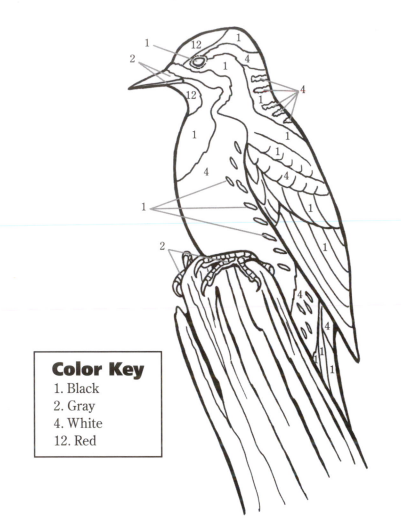

Color Key
1. Black
2. Gray
4. White
12. Red

SIZE: _____ "

○ 17½" or larger

○ 17" (crow size)

○ 11–16½"

○ 9–10½" (robin size)

○ 7–8½"

○ 5-6½" (sparrow size)

○ Less than 5"

FACTS / NOTES:

1. _____

_____

2. _____

_____

3. _____

_____

4. _____

_____

5. _____

_____

Range: At what time of year are you most likely to find this bird in your area?

A. Summer   **B.** Winter   **C.** All Year   **D.** Never

In which habitat is this bird most likely to nest?

☐ **Woodland**

☐ **Grassland**

☐ **Wetland**

Draw a nearby spot where you might see this bird.

56

HOUSE WREN *Troglodytes aedon*

⬜ Check the box after you have seen this bird.

Color Key
1. Black
2. Gray
4. White
6. Light Yellow
7. Dark Brown
8. Brown
9. Tan

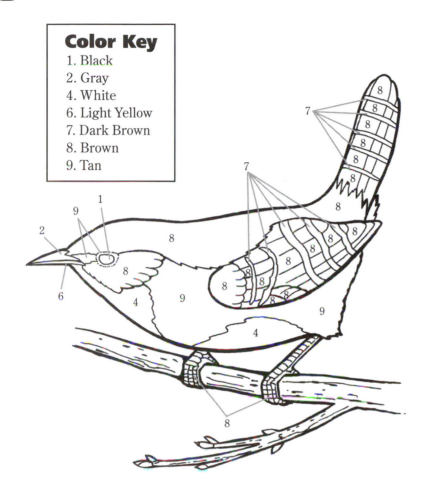

SIZE: _____ "

○ 17½" or larger

○ 17" (crow size)

○ 11–16½"

○ 9–10½" (robin size)

○ 7–8½"

○ 5-6½" (sparrow size)

○ Less than 5"

FACTS/NOTES:

1. _____

_____

2. _____

_____

3. _____

_____

4. _____

_____

5. _____

_____

Range: At what time of year are you most likely to find this bird in your area?

A. Summer   **B.** Winter   **C.** All Year   **D.** Never

In which habitat is this bird most likely to nest?

Draw a nearby spot where you might see this bird.

⬜ **Woodland**

⬜ **Grassland**

⬜ **Wetland**

VOCABULARY

Conifer: A type of tree that bears its seeds in a cone. Most conifers have green needles that remain on the tree year-round. Northwoods conifers include Balsam Fir, Eastern White Pine, Red Pine, Black Spruce, White Spruce and White Cedar.

Deciduous: A tree that usually sheds all of its leaves in autumn, such as Paper Birch, Sugar Maple or White Oak.

Field Markings: Noticeable marks on the body of a bird. Markings may include colorful patches, stripes and ring patterns on a bird's feathers.

Grassland: A prairie-like type of habitat dominated by grasses and wildflowers.

Habitat: The local environment in which a bird lives. Must provide food, water, cover (shelter) and space.

Migration: Seasonal movements from one area to another, often triggered by the length of daylight hours, weather or food availability.

Range: The particular geographic region in which a species is found.

Territory: The area a bird (often the male of the species) will defend, usually during breeding season, against intruders of its own species.

Wetland: A marshy type of habitat that has wet or water-covered soil and plants adapted to living in wet conditions. Includes swamps, bogs and the shores of lakes and rivers.

Woodland: Habitat dominated by deciduous or coniferous trees.

ATTRACT BIRDS TO YOUR BACKYARD

Feeding the birds is a fun way to attract them to your backyard. You can arrange and fill feeders based on the season and dietary needs of your feathered friends, but it's possible to get started with one basic feeding station. Place the feeder 10 to 12 feet from a tree or shrub and fill it with black oil sunflower seed. It may take a couple of days for birds to find the new feeder, but you'll soon have many different visitors.

Birdhouses provide nesting areas for a variety of species, and allow you to observe birds' courtship, territorial and parenting behaviors. You can put a birdhouse on a post, in a tree or even on a tool shed. Most birds prefer a house that's 4 to 10 feet above the ground. Make sure the door faces north or south, not east or west (to keep the sun from shining inside) and clean the house each year in the fall or early spring.

BIRD SIZES AND HABITATS

Bird Species	Size	Habitat
American Crow	17"	Woodlands
American Goldfinch	5"	Grasslands
American Redstart	5"	Woodlands
American Robin	9–10½"	Woodlands
American Tree Sparrow	6"	Grasslands
Baltimore Oriole	7–8"	Woodlands
Barn Swallow	7"	Grasslands
Belted Kingfisher	13"	Wetlands
Black-capped Chickadee	5"	Woodlands
Blue Jay	12"	Woodlands
Bobolink	7"	Grasslands
Brown Creeper	5"	Woodlands
Cedar Waxwing	7½"	Woodlands
Common Grackle	12"	Grasslands
Common Raven	22–27"	Woodlands
Common Yellowthroat	5"	Wetlands
Chipping Sparrow	5"	Woodlands
Dark-eyed Junco	5½"	Woodlands
Downy Woodpecker	6"	Woodlands
Eastern Bluebird	7"	Grasslands
Eastern Kingbird	8"	Grasslands
Eastern Meadowlark	9"	Grasslands
Eastern Phoebe	7"	Woodlands
Eastern Towhee	7–8"	Woodlands
Eastern Wood Pewee	6½"	Woodlands
Evening Grosbeak	8"	Woodlands
Gray Catbird	9"	Woodlands
Hairy Woodpecker	9"	Woodlands
House Finch	5"	Woodlands
House Sparrow	6"	Woodlands
House Wren	5"	Woodlands
Killdeer	11"	Wetlands
Mourning Dove	12"	Woodlands
Northern Cardinal	8½"	Woodlands
Northern Flicker	12"	Woodlands
Pileated Woodpecker	19"	Woodlands
Purple Finch	6"	Woodlands
Purple Martin	8½"	Grasslands
Red-breasted Nuthatch	4½"	Woodlands
Red Crossbill	6½"	Woodlands
Red-headed Woodpecker	9"	Woodlands
Red-winged Blackbird	8½"	Wetlands
Rose-breasted Grosbeak	7–8"	Woodlands
Ruby-throated Hummingbird	3–3½"	Woodlands
Scarlet Tanager	7"	Woodlands
Tree Swallow	5–6"	Woodlands
White-breasted Nuthatch	5–6"	Woodlands
Yellow-bellied Sapsucker	8½"	Woodlands
Yellow Warbler	5"	Woodlands
Yellow-rumped Warbler	5–6"	Woodlands

SEASONAL BIRD LOCATION

Species	Connecticut	Maine	Massachusetts
American Crow	Year-round	Summer (North)/ Year-round (South)	Year-round
American Goldfinch	Year-round	Year-round	Year-round
American Redstart	Summer	Summer	Summer
American Robin	Summer (North)/ Year-round (South)	Summer (North)/ Year-round (South)	Year-round
American Tree Sparrow	Winter	Winter	Winter
Baltimore Oriole	Summer	Summer	Summer
Barn Swallow	Summer	Summer	Summer
Belted Kingfisher	Summer / Year-round (Coast)	Summer / Year-round (Coast)	Summer / Year-round (Coast)
Black-capped Chickadee	Year-round	Year-round	Year-round
Blue Jay	Year-round	Year-round	Year-round
Bobolink	Summer	Summer	Summer
Brown Creeper	Year-round	Year-round	Year-round
Cedar Waxwing	Year-round	Summer (North)/ Year-round (South)	Year-round
Chipping Sparrow	Summer	Summer	Summer
Common Grackle	Summer / Year-round (Coast)	Summer	Summer
Common Raven	-	Year-round	-
Common Yellowthroat	Summer	Summer	Summer
Dark-eyed Junco	Winter / Year-round	Year-round	Year-round (West)/ Winter (East)
Downy Woodpecker	Year-round	Year-round	Year-round
Eastern Phoebe	Summer	Summer	Summer
Eastern Bluebird	Summer / Year-round (Coast)	Summer / Year-round (Coast)	Year-round
Eastern Kingbird	Summer	Summer	Summer
Eastern Meadowlark	Summer (North)/ Year-round (South)	Summer	Summer / Year-round (Coast)
Eastern Towhee	Summer / Year-round (Coast)	Summer	Summer
Eastern Wood Pewee	Summer	Summer	Summer
Evening Grosbeak	Winter	Year-round	Winter
Gray Catbird	Summer	Summer	Summer / Year-round (Coast)
Hairy Woodpecker	Year-round	Year-round	Year-round
House Finch	Year-round	Year-round	Year-round
House Sparrow	Year-round	Year-round	Year-round
House Wren	Summer	Summer	Summer
Killdeer	Summer / Year-round (Coast)	Summer	Summer
Mourning Dove	Year-round	Summer (Central)/ Year-round (South)	Year-round
Northern Cardinal	Year-round	Year-round	Year-round
Northern Flicker	Summer / Year-round (Coast)	Summer / Year-round (Coast)	Summer (West)/ Year-round (East)
Pileated Woodpecker	Year-round	Year-round	Year-round
Purple Finch	Year-round (North)/ Winter (South)	Year-round	Year-round
Purple Martin	Summer	Summer	Summer
Red Crossbill	Year-round	Year-round	Year-round
Red-breasted Nuthatch	Year-round / Winter	Year-round	Year-round
Red-headed Woodpecker	Summer	-	Migratory
Red-winged Blackbird	Summer / Year-round (Coast)	Summer	Summer
Rose-breasted Grosbeak	Summer	Summer	Summer
Ruby-throated Hummingbird	Summer	Summer	Summer
Scarlet Tanager	Summer	Summer	Summer
Tree Swallow	Summer	Summer	Summer
White-breasted Nuthatch	Year-round	Year-round	Year-round
Yellow Warbler	Summer	Summer	Summer
Yellow-bellied Sapsucker	Summer	Summer	Summer
Yellow-Rumped Warbler	Summer / Winter (Coast)	Summer / Year-round (Coast)	Summer (West)/ Winter (Coast)

The information noted here is true for most areas of the Northwoods. However, migration patterns may be different in your area.

Michigan	Minnesota	New Hampshire
Year-round	Year-round	Year-round
Summer (North)/ Year-round (South)	Summer (North)/ Year-round (South)	Year-round
Summer	Summer	Summer
Summer	Summer / Year-round (South)	Summer / Year-round (Southeast)
Winter	Winter	Winter
Summer	Summer	Summer
Summer	Summer	Summer
Summer	Summer / Year-round (Southeast)	Summer / Year-round (Coast)
Year-round	Year-round	Year-round
Year-round	Year-round	Year-round
Summer	Summer	Summer
Year-round	Summer (North)/ Year-round (South)	Year-round
Summer (North)/ Year-round (South)	Summer (North)/ Year-round (South)	Year-round
Summer	Summer	Summer
Summer	Summer / Year-round (South)	Summer (North)/ Year-round (South)
Year-round	Year-round	Year-round (North)
Summer	Summer	Summer
Year-round (North)/ Winter (South)	Winter (South)/ Summer (North)	Year-round
Year-round	Year-round	Year-round
Summer	Summer	Summer
Summer	Summer	Summer / Year-round (South)
Summer	Summer	Summer
Summer	Summer	Summer
Summer	Summer	Summer
Summer	Summer	Summer
Year-round (North)/ Winter (Central)	Year-round / Winter (Central)	Year-round
Summer	Summer	Summer
Year-round	Year-round	Year-round
Year-round	Year-round	Year-round
Year-round	Year-round	Year-round
Summer	Summer	Summer
Summer	Summer	Summer
Summer (North)/ Year-round (South)	Summer (North)/ Year-round (South)	Summer
Year-round	Year-round	Year-round
Summer (North)/ Year-round (South)	Summer / Year-round (South)	Summer
Year-round	Year-round	Year-round
Year-round (North)/ Winter (South)	Summer (North)/ Year-round (Central)	Year-round
Summer	Summer	Summer
Year-round (North)	Winter (Northeast)/ Year-round (North)	Year-round
Year-round (North)/ Winter (South)	Year-round (North)/ Winter (South)	Year-round
Summer (Central)/ Year-round (South)	Summer	-
Summer	Summer / Year-round (South)	Summer (North)/ Year-round (South)
Summer	Summer	Summer
Summer	Summer	Summer
Summer	Summer	Summer
Summer	Summer	Summer
Year-round	Year-round	Year-round
Summer	Summer	Summer
Summer	Summer	Summer
Summer	Summer	Summer

Species	New Jersey	New York	Pennsylvania
American Crow	Year-round	Year-round	Year-round
American Goldfinch	Year-round	Year-round	Year-round
American Redstart	Summer	Summer	Summer
American Robin	Year-round	Summer (Northeast)/ Year-round	Year-round
American Tree Sparrow	Winter	Winter	Winter
Baltimore Oriole	Summer	Summer	Summer
Barn Swallow	Summer	Summer	Summer
Belted Kingfisher	Year-round	Summer	Summer / Year-round (East)
Black-capped Chickadee	Year-round (North)	Year-round	Year-round
Blue Jay	Year-round	Year-round	Year-round
Bobolink	Summer	Summer	Summer
Brown Creeper	Year-round (North)/ Winter (South)	Year-round	Year-round (North)/ Winter (South)
Cedar Waxwing	Summer (North)/ Year-round (South)	Year-round	Year-round
Chipping Sparrow	Summer	Summer	Summer
Common Grackle	Year-round	Summer	Year-round
Common Raven	-	Year-round	Year-round
Common Yellowthroat	Summer	Summer	Summer
Dark-eyed Junco	Year-round (Northwest)/ Winter	Year-round (East)/ Winter (West)	Year-round (North)/ Winter (South)
Downy Woodpecker	Year-round	Year-round	Year-round
Eastern Phoebe	Summer	Summer	Summer
Eastern Bluebird	Year-round	Year-round (West/East)/ Summer (Central)	Year-round
Eastern Kingbird	Summer	Summer	Summer
Eastern Meadowlark	Summer (North)/ Year-round (South)	Year-round (Southwest)/ Summer (Southeast)	Summer / Year-round (Southeast)
Eastern Towhee	Summer (North)/ Year-round (South)	Summer	Summer / Year-round (Southeast)
Eastern Wood Pewee	Summer	Summer	Summer
Evening Grosbeak	Winter (North)	Winter / Year-round (Northeast)	Winter
Gray Catbird	Summer / Year-round (Southeast)	Summer / Year-round (Coast)	Summer
Hairy Woodpecker	Year-round	Year-round	Year-round
House Finch	Year-round	Year-round	Year-round
House Sparrow	Year-round	Year-round	Year-round
House Wren	Summer	Summer	Summer
Killdeer	Summer / Year-round (Southeast)	Summer / Year-round (Coast)	Summer / Year-round (Southeast)
Mourning Dove	Year-round	Year-round	Year-round
Northern Cardinal	Year-round	Year-round	Year-round
Northern Flicker	Year-round	Year-round	Year-round
Pileated Woodpecker	Year-round	Year-round	Year-round
Purple Finch	Year-round (North)/ Winter (South)	Year-round (North) / Winter (South)	Year-round (North)/ Winter (Southea
Purple Martin	Summer	Summer	Summer
Red Crossbill	-	Year-round (East)/ Winter (West)	Year-round (Northwest)
Red-breasted Nuthatch	Year-round (North)/ Winter (South)	Year-round /Winter	Year-round (North)/ Winter (South)
Red-headed Woodpecker	Summer	Year-round	Summer / Year-round (Southeast)
Red-winged Blackbird	Year-round	Year-round	Summer / Year-round (Southwest)
Rose-breasted Grosbeak	Summer	Summer	Summer
Ruby-throated Hummingbird	Summer	Summer	Summer
Scarlet Tanager	Summer	Summer	Summer
Tree Swallow	Summer	Summer	Summer
White-breasted Nuthatch	Year-round	Year-round	Year-round
Yellow Warbler	Summer	Summer	Summer
Yellow-bellied Sapsucker	Winter	Summer	Summer
Yellow-Rumped Warbler	Summer (North)/ Winter	Year-round	Summer / Winter (Northwest)

The information noted here is true for most areas of the Northwoods. However, migration patterns may be different in your area.

Vermont	Wisconsin
Year-round	Year-round
Year-round	Year-round
Summer	Summer
Summer	Summer
Winter	Winter
Summer	Summer
Summer	Summer
Summer	Summer (North)/ Year-round (South)
Year-round	Year-round
Year-round	Year-round
Summer	Summer
Year-round	Year-round (North)/ Winter (South)
Year-round	Year-round
Summer	Summer
Summer (North)/ Year-round (South)	Summer
Year-round (North)	Year-round
Summer	Summer
Year-round	Year-round (North)/ Winter (South)
Year-round	Year-round
Summer	Summer
Summer / Year-round (South)	Summer
Summer	Summer
Summer	Summer
Summer	Summer
Summer	Summer
Year-round	Year-round (North)/ Winter (Central)
Summer	Summer
Year-round	Year-round
Year-round	Year-round
Year-round	Year-round
Summer	Summer
Summer	Summer
Summer	Summer (North)/ Year-round (South)
Year-round	Year-round
Summer	Summer
Year-round	Year-round
Year-round	Year-round (North)/ Winter (South)
Summer	Summer
Year-round	Year-round (North)/ Winter (South)
Year-round	Year-round (North)/ Winter (South)
-	Summer
Summer (North)/ Year-round (South)	Summer
Summer	Summer
Summer	Summer
Summer	Summer
Summer	Summer
Year-round	Year-round
Summer	Summer
Summer	Summer
Summer	Summer

OTHER BIRD RESOURCES

About Birds of the Northwoods

Cornell Lab of Ornithology. "All About Birds: Bird Guide."
http://www.birds.cornell.edu/AllAboutBirds/BirdGuide, 2003.

Henderson, Carrol L. *Wild About Birds: the DNR Feeding Guide*.
St. Paul, MN: Minnesota's Bookstore, 1995.

National Wildlife Federation. "Field Guides." eNature: America's Wildlife
Resource, http://www.enature.com/fieldguides, 2005.

Stokes, Donald W. and Lillian Q. Stokes. *Stokes Guide to Bird Behavior, Volumes 1–3*.
New York: Little, Brown & Company, 1979 and 1983.

Tekiela, Stan. *Birds of...* field guides. Cambridge, MN: Adventure Publications, Inc.,
(www.adventurepublications.net), 2000–2005.

Attracting Birds to Your Area

Cornell Lab of Ornithology. "All About Birds: Attracting Birds."
http://www.birds.cornell.edu/AllAboutBirds/attracting, 2003.

Dennis, John V. and Michael McKinley. *How to Attract Birds*. San Ramon, CA: Ortho Books, 1995.

Dobson, Clive. *Feeding Wild Birds in Winter*. Willowdale, Ontario: Firefly Books Ltd., 1994.

Henderson, Carrol L. *Wild About Birds: the DNR Feeding Guide*.
St. Paul, MN: Minnesota's Bookstore, 1995.

Roth, Sally. *Attracting Birds to Your Backyard: 536 Ways to Create a Haven for Your Favorite Birds*.
Emmaus, PA: Rodale Press, Inc., 1998.

Stokes, Donald W. and Lillian Q. Stokes. *The Complete Birdhouse Book*.
New York: Little, Brown & Company, 1990.

ABOUT THE AUTHOR

David Grack is a biology teacher who has inspired students from kindergarten to twelfth grade. He helps youngsters appreciate the diversity and complexity of our natural surroundings. David earned his Bachelor of Arts Degree in Biology from St. Olaf College (Northfield, Minnesota) and a Master of Arts Degree in Education, Natural Sciences and Environmental Education from Hamline University (St. Paul, Minnesota). In addition to bird watching, David enjoys camping, canoeing, snowshoeing and fishing. He shares his enthusiasm for nature and outdoor recreation with everyone he meets. He resides in Buffalo, Minnesota, with his wife, Jodi, and their children.